FEARFUL AVOIDANT ATTACHMENT WORKBOOK

Rebuild Healthy Patterns for Safe and Meaningful Relationships

BY
DARIO JEYCO

COPYRIGHT © 2023

EXPOSURE THERAPY
FOR
EMOTIONAL CLOSENESS

Individuals with fearful avoidant attachment may struggle to get close to others, feel inferior to themselves and have a negative view of others.

They may avoid emotional intimacy because they see this as a threat. As someone who wants to regain their emotional balance through these exercises, try to engage in low-risk, casual interactions with others. This could mean saying hello to a neighbor or co-worker, or making small talk with a stranger.

About gradually increasing the level of intimacy over time.

	TASK ACCOMPLISHED ☐ intimacy level ○ ○ ○ ○ ○
	TASK ACCOMPLISHED ☐ intimacy level ○ ○ ○ ○ ○
	TASK ACCOMPLISHED ☐ intimacy level ○ ○ ○ ○ ○

NOTES

....

....

OVERCOMING FEARFUL AVOIDANT ATTACHMENT WORKSHEET

This table will help you examine the impact of the repercussions of the fearful avoidant attachment style on your social interactions on a daily, weekly or monthly basis... The aim of this paper is to develop an appropriate coping plan to control negative signs if you want to bring about real change in your personality.

FEARFUL AVOIDANT ATTACHMENT TAGS AND TRAITS	What are the characteristics of a fearful avoidant attachment style that you experience today? Describe how this affected your dealings.
	👍 WHAT WAS SO COOL: ✋ WHAT WAS WRONG:

AVOIDANT ATTACHMENT WORKSHEET -DBT-

START YOUR DAY MINDFULLY WITH A FEW MINUTES OF MEDITATION OR MINDFULNESS. THIS PRACTICE WILL HELP YOU FEEL CENTERED, ENHANCE SELF-AWARENESS, AND ESTABLISH A POSITIVE MINDSET FOR THE DAY.
TAKE A MOMENT TO REFLECT ON YOUR EMOTIONS AND EMOTIONAL STATE. ASK YOURSELF ABOUT YOUR FEELINGS, THOUGHTS, AND ANY ATTACHMENT-RELATED PATTERNS YOU MIGHT OBSERVE.
EMBRACE POSITIVE AFFIRMATIONS THAT FOSTER TRUST, VULNERABILITY, AND EMOTIONAL CONNECTION. REPEAT PHRASES LIKE "I AM DESERVING OF LOVE AND CONNECTION," "I AM OPEN TO EMOTIONAL INTIMACY," OR "I CAN CONFIDE IN OTHERS WITH MY FEELINGS."

⊘ ___ : ___

⊘ ___ : ___

Daily Wins

Mood Tracking ✔

- ANGRY ☐
- ANNOYED ☐
- ANXIOUS ☐
- ASHAMED ☐
- EMBARRASSING ☐
- COURAGEOUS ☐
- CALM ☐
- CHEERFUL ☐
- COLD ☐
- CONFUSED ☐
- DISCOURAGED ☐
- DISTRACTED ☐
- EMBARRASSED ☐
- EXCITED ☐
- FRIENDLY ☐
- GUILTY ☐
- HAPPY ☐
- HOPEFUL ☐
- SOLITARY ☐
- BELOVED ☐
- NERVOUS ☐
- OFFENDED ☐
- AFRAID ☐
- THOUGHTFUL ☐
- TIRED OUT ☐
- UNCOMFORTABLE ☐
- UNCERTAIN ☐

DAILY MOOD CYCLE

Instructions: Think about your day from start to finish. Color the first square to express your feelings each time of the day. Next, write a word that reflects your feelings, and draw in the circle a picture of your face that reflects your feelings at that moment.

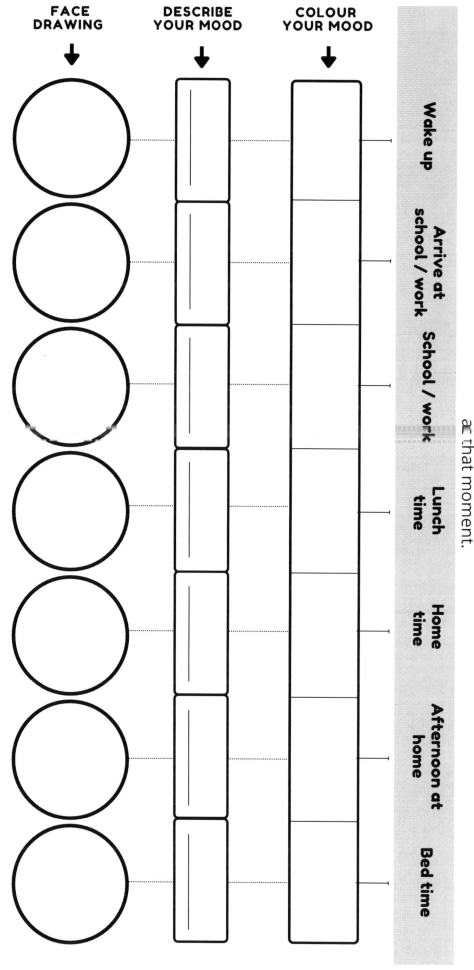

FACE DRAWING

DESCRIBE YOUR MOOD

COLOUR YOUR MOOD

Wake up

Arrive at school / work

School / work

Lunch time

Home time

Afternoon at home

Bed time

AVOIDANT ATTACHMENT WORKSHEET

Date : _____

DAILY / WEEKLY - DBT WORKSHEET (OPTIONAL)

- List three emotions that surfaced throughout yesterday. Reflect on how each emotion affected my interactions and decisions.
- Write a kind and supportive message to myself, focusing on self-acceptance and understanding.
- What are the prospects that will make you give up the difficulty of trusting others and open up.
- Write down one boundary I can set today to prioritize my emotional well-being.
- Write down any lingering worries or thoughts before bedtime, and consider ways to ease them.

All about your journey towards changing your negative beliefs about having new romantic relationships.

_____

_____

_____

_____

_____

_____

_____

_____

_____

_____

_____

_____

_____

_____

_____

DATE :   /   /

EXPOSURE THERAPY
FOR
EMOTIONAL CLOSENESS

Individuals with fearful avoidant attachment may struggle to get close to others, feel inferior to themselves and have a negative view of others.

    They may avoid emotional intimacy because they see this as a threat. As someone who wants to regain their emotional balance through these exercises, try to engage in low-risk, casual interactions with others. This could mean saying hello to a neighbor or co-worker, or making small talk with a stranger.

About gradually increasing the level of intimacy over time.

	TASK ACCOMPLISHED ☐ intimacy level ○ ○ ○ ○ ○
	TASK ACCOMPLISHED ☐ intimacy level ○ ○ ○ ○ ○
	TASK ACCOMPLISHED ☐ intimacy level ○ ○ ○ ○ ○

NOTES

....

....

OVERCOMING FEARFUL AVOIDANT ATTACHMENT WORKSHEET

This table will help you examine the impact of the repercussions of the fearful avoidant attachment style on your social interactions on a daily, weekly or monthly basis... The aim of this paper is to develop an appropriate coping plan to control negative signs if you want to bring about real change in your personality.

FEARFUL AVOIDANT ATTACHMENT TAGS AND TRAITS	What are the characteristics of a fearful avoidant attachment style that you experience today? Describe how this affected your dealings.
	👍 WHAT WAS SO COOL: ✋ WHAT WAS WRONG:

AVOIDANT ATTACHMENT WORKSHEET -DBT-

START YOUR DAY MINDFULLY WITH A FEW MINUTES OF MEDITATION OR MINDFULNESS. THIS PRACTICE WILL HELP YOU FEEL CENTERED, ENHANCE SELF-AWARENESS, AND ESTABLISH A POSITIVE MINDSET FOR THE DAY.
TAKE A MOMENT TO REFLECT ON YOUR EMOTIONS AND EMOTIONAL STATE. ASK YOURSELF ABOUT YOUR FEELINGS, THOUGHTS, AND ANY ATTACHMENT-RELATED PATTERNS YOU MIGHT OBSERVE.
EMBRACE POSITIVE AFFIRMATIONS THAT FOSTER TRUST, VULNERABILITY, AND EMOTIONAL CONNECTION. REPEAT PHRASES LIKE "I AM DESERVING OF LOVE AND CONNECTION," "I AM OPEN TO EMOTIONAL INTIMACY," OR "I CAN CONFIDE IN OTHERS WITH MY FEELINGS."

⊘ ___ : ___

⊘ ___ : ___

Daily Wins

Mood Tracking

- ANGRY ☐
- ANNOYED ☐
- ANXIOUS ☐
- ASHAMED ☐
- EMBARRASSING ☐
- COURAGEOUS ☐
- CALM ☐
- CHEERFUL ☐
- COLD ☐
- CONFUSED ☐
- DISCOURAGED ☐
- DISTRACTED ☐
- EMBARRASSED ☐
- EXCITED ☐
- FRIENDLY ☐
- GUILTY ☐
- HAPPY ☐
- HOPEFUL ☐
- SOLITARY ☐
- BELOVED ☐
- NERVOUS ☐
- OFFENDED ☐
- AFRAID ☐
- THOUGHTFUL ☐
- TIRED OUT ☐
- UNCOMFORTABLE ☐
- UNCERTAIN ☐

DAILY MOOD CYCLE

Instructions: Think about your day from start to finish. Color the first square to express your feelings each time of the day. Next, write a word that reflects your feelings, and draw in the circle a picture of your face that reflects your feelings at that moment.

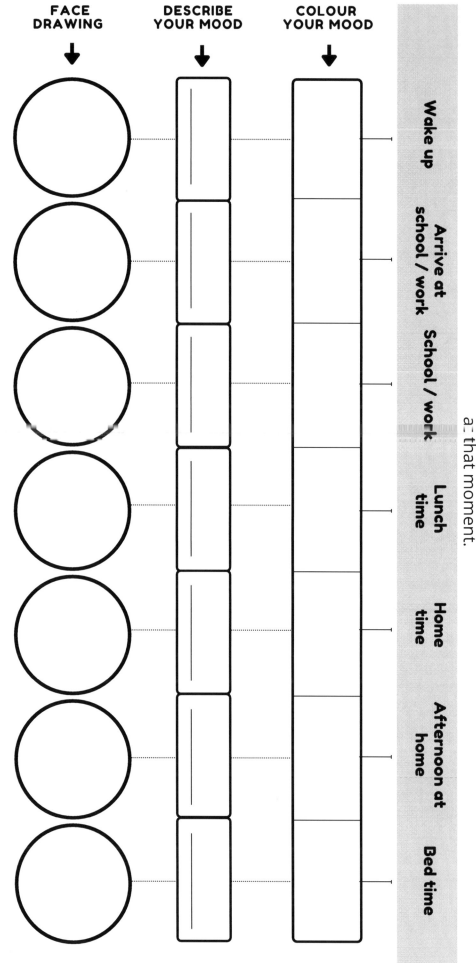

	FACE DRAWING	DESCRIBE YOUR MOOD	COLOUR YOUR MOOD
Wake up			
Arrive at school / work			
School / work			
Lunch time			
Home time			
Afternoon at home			
Bed time			

AVOIDANT ATTACHMENT WORKSHEET

Date : _____

DAILY / WEEKLY - DBT WORKSHEET (OPTIONAL)

- List three emotions that surfaced throughout yesterday. Reflect on how each emotion affected my interactions and decisions.
- Write a kind and supportive message to myself, focusing on self-acceptance and understanding.
- What are the prospects that will make you give up the difficulty of trusting others and open up.
- Write down one boundary I can set today to prioritize my emotional well-being.
- Write down any lingering worries or thoughts before bedtime, and consider ways to ease them.

All about your journey towards changing your negative beliefs about having new romantic relationships.

_____

_____

_____

_____

_____

_____

_____

_____

_____

_____

_____

_____

_____

_____

_____

DATE :   /   /

EXPOSURE THERAPY FOR EMOTIONAL CLOSENESS

Individuals with fearful avoidant attachment may struggle to get close to others, feel inferior to themselves and have a negative view of others.

They may avoid emotional intimacy because they see this as a threat. As someone who wants to regain their emotional balance through these exercises, try to engage in low-risk, casual interactions with others. This could mean saying hello to a neighbor or co-worker, or making small talk with a stranger.

About gradually increasing the level of intimacy over time.

	TASK ACCOMPLISHED □ intimacy level ○ ○ ○ ○ ○
	TASK ACCOMPLISHED □ intimacy level ○ ○ ○ ○ ○
	TASK ACCOMPLISHED □ intimacy level ○ ○ ○ ○ ○

NOTES

....

....

OVERCOMING FEARFUL AVOIDANT ATTACHMENT WORKSHEET

This table will help you examine the impact of the repercussions of the fearful avoidant attachment style on your social interactions on a daily, weekly or monthly basis... The aim of this paper is to develop an appropriate coping plan to control negative signs if you want to bring about real change in your personality.

FEARFUL AVOIDANT ATTACHMENT TAGS AND TRAITS	What are the characteristics of a fearful avoidant attachment style that you experience today? Describe how this affected your dealings.
	👍 WHAT WAS SO COOL:
	✋ WHAT WAS WRONG:

AVOIDANT ATTACHMENT WORKSHEET -DBT-

Date: / /

Sleep Quality :

START YOUR DAY MINDFULLY WITH A FEW MINUTES OF MEDITATION OR MINDFULNESS. THIS PRACTICE WILL HELP YOU FEEL CENTERED, ENHANCE SELF-AWARENESS, AND ESTABLISH A POSITIVE MINDSET FOR THE DAY.
TAKE A MOMENT TO REFLECT ON YOUR EMOTIONS AND EMOTIONAL STATE. ASK YOURSELF ABOUT YOUR FEELINGS, THOUGHTS, AND ANY ATTACHMENT-RELATED PATTERNS YOU MIGHT OBSERVE.
EMBRACE POSITIVE AFFIRMATIONS THAT FOSTER TRUST, VULNERABILITY, AND EMOTIONAL CONNECTION. REPEAT PHRASES LIKE "I AM DESERVING OF LOVE AND CONNECTION," "I AM OPEN TO EMOTIONAL INTIMACY," OR "I CAN CONFIDE IN OTHERS WITH MY FEELINGS."

✓ ___ : ___

✓ ___ : ___

Mood Tracking ✓

- ANGRY ☐
- ANNOYED ☐
- ANXIOUS ☐
- ASHAMED ☐
- EMBARRASSING ☐
- COURAGEOUS ☐
- CALM ☐
- CHEERFUL ☐
- COLD ☐
- CONFUSED ☐
- DISCOURAGED ☐
- DISTRACTED ☐
- EMBARRASSED ☐
- EXCITED ☐
- FRIENDLY ☐
- GUILTY ☐
- HAPPY ☐
- HOPEFUL ☐
- SOLITARY ☐
- BELOVED ☐
- NERVOUS ☐
- OFFENDED ☐
- AFRAID ☐
- THOUGHTFUL ☐
- TIRED OUT ☐
- UNCOMFORTABLE ☐
- UNCERTAIN ☐

Daily Wins

DAILY MOOD CYCLE

Instructions: Think about your day from start to finish. Color the first square to express your feelings each time of the day. Next, write a word that reflects your feelings, and draw in the circle a picture of your face that reflects your feelings at that moment.

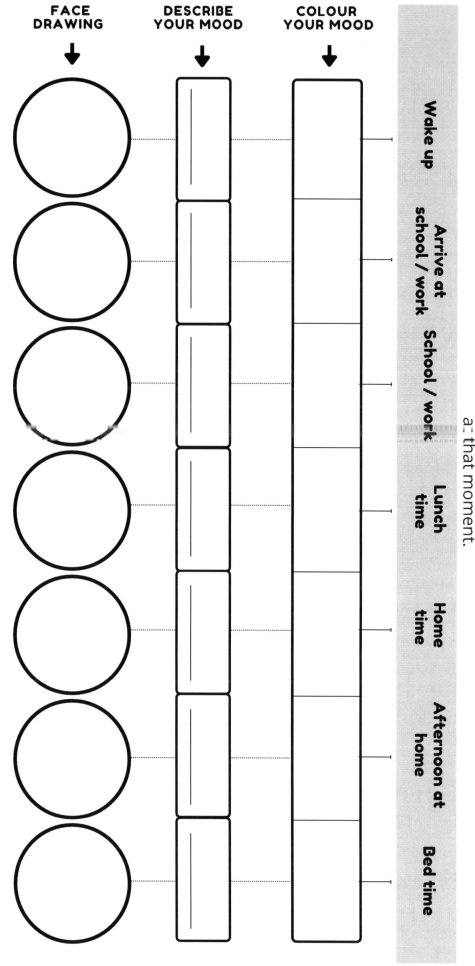

FACE DRAWING

DESCRIBE YOUR MOOD

COLOUR YOUR MOOD

Wake up

Arrive at school / work

School / work

Lunch time

Home time

Afternoon at home

Bed time

AVOIDANT ATTACHMENT WORKSHEET

[OPEN]

Date : _____

DAILY / WEEKLY - DBT WORKSHEET (OPTIONAL)

- List three emotions that surfaced throughout yesterday. Reflect on how each emotion affected my interactions and decisions.
- Write a kind and supportive message to myself, focusing on self-acceptance and understanding.
- What are the prospects that will make you give up the difficulty of trusting others and open up.
- Write down one boundary I can set today to prioritize my emotional well-being.
- Write down any lingering worries or thoughts before bedtime, and consider ways to ease them.

All about your journey towards changing your negative beliefs about having new romantic relationships.

_____

_____

_____

_____

_____

_____

_____

_____

_____

_____

_____

_____

_____

_____

_____

_____

DATE :   /   /

EXPOSURE THERAPY FOR EMOTIONAL CLOSENESS

Individuals with fearful avoidant attachment may struggle to get close to others, feel inferior to themselves and have a negative view of others.

    They may avoid emotional intimacy because they see this as a threat. As someone who wants to regain their emotional balance through these exercises, try to engage in low-risk, casual interactions with others. This could mean saying hello to a neighbor or co-worker, or making small talk with a stranger.

About gradually increasing the level of intimacy over time.

	TASK ACCOMPLISHED ☐ intimacy level ○ ○ ○ ○ ○
	TASK ACCOMPLISHED ☐ intimacy level ○ ○ ○ ○ ○
	TASK ACCOMPLISHED ☐ intimacy level ○ ○ ○ ○ ○

NOTES

....

....

DATE :   /   /

OVERCOMING FEARFUL AVOIDANT ATTACHMENT WORKSHEET

This table will help you examine the impact of the repercussions of the fearful avoidant attachment style on your social interactions on a daily, weekly or monthly basis... The aim of this paper is to develop an appropriate coping plan to control negative signs if you want to bring about real change in your personality.

FEARFUL AVOIDANT ATTACHMENT TAGS AND TRAITS	What are the characteristics of a fearful avoidant attachment style that you experience today? Describe how this affected your dealings.
	👍 WHAT WAS SO COOL:
	✋ WHAT WAS WRONG:

AVOIDANT ATTACHMENT WORKSHEET -DBT-

Date: / /

Sleep Quality :

START YOUR DAY MINDFULLY WITH A FEW MINUTES OF MEDITATION OR MINDFULNESS. THIS PRACTICE WILL HELP YOU FEEL CENTERED, ENHANCE SELF-AWARENESS, AND ESTABLISH A POSITIVE MINDSET FOR THE DAY.
TAKE A MOMENT TO REFLECT ON YOUR EMOTIONS AND EMOTIONAL STATE. ASK YOURSELF ABOUT YOUR FEELINGS, THOUGHTS, AND ANY ATTACHMENT-RELATED PATTERNS YOU MIGHT OBSERVE.
EMBRACE POSITIVE AFFIRMATIONS THAT FOSTER TRUST, VULNERABILITY, AND EMOTIONAL CONNECTION. REPEAT PHRASES LIKE "I AM DESERVING OF LOVE AND CONNECTION," "I AM OPEN TO EMOTIONAL INTIMACY," OR "I CAN CONFIDE IN OTHERS WITH MY FEELINGS."

✓ ___ : ___

✓ ___ : ___

Daily Wins

Mood Tracking ✓

ANGRY ☐
ANNOYED ☐
ANXIOUS ☐
ASHAMED ☐
EMBARRASSING ☐
COURAGEOUS ☐
CALM ☐
CHEERFUL ☐
COLD ☐
CONFUSED ☐
DISCOURAGED ☐
DISTRACTED ☐
EMBARRASSED ☐
EXCITED ☐
FRIENDLY ☐
GUILTY ☐
HAPPY ☐
HOPEFUL ☐
SOLITARY ☐
BELOVED ☐
NERVOUS ☐
OFFENDED ☐
AFRAID ☐
THOUGHTFUL ☐
TIRED OUT ☐
UNCOMFORTABLE ☐
UNCERTAIN ☐

DAILY MOOD CYCLE

Instructions: Think about your day from start to finish. Color the first square to express your feelings each time of the day. Next, write a word that reflects your feelings, and draw in the circle a picture of your face that reflects your feelings at that moment.

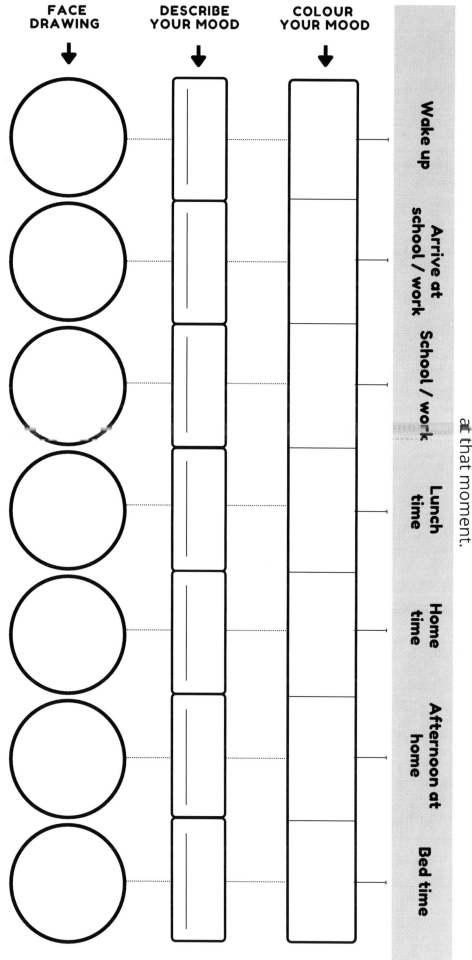

FACE DRAWING

DESCRIBE YOUR MOOD

COLOUR YOUR MOOD

Wake up

Arrive at school / work

School / work

Lunch time

Home time

Afternoon at home

Bed time

AVOIDANT ATTACHMENT WORKSHEET

Date : _____

DAILY / WEEKLY - DBT WORKSHEET (OPTIONAL)

- List three emotions that surfaced throughout yesterday. Reflect on how each emotion affected my interactions and decisions.
- Write a kind and supportive message to myself, focusing on self-acceptance and understanding.
- What are the prospects that will make you give up the difficulty of trusting others and open up.
- Write down one boundary I can set today to prioritize my emotional well-being.
- Write down any lingering worries or thoughts before bedtime, and consider ways to ease them.

All about your journey towards changing your negative beliefs about having new romantic relationships.

_____

_____

_____

_____

_____

_____

_____

_____

_____

_____

_____

_____

_____

_____

_____

_____

_____

DATE :   /   /

EXPOSURE THERAPY FOR EMOTIONAL CLOSENESS

Individuals with fearful avoidant attachment may struggle to get close to others, feel inferior to themselves and have a negative view of others.

    They may avoid emotional intimacy because they see this as a threat. As someone who wants to regain their emotional balance through these exercises, try to engage in low-risk, casual interactions with others. This could mean saying hello to a neighbor or co-worker, or making small talk with a stranger.

About gradually increasing the level of intimacy over time.

	TASK ACCOMPLISHED ☐ intimacy level ○ ○ ○ ○ ○
	TASK ACCOMPLISHED ☐ intimacy level ○ ○ ○ ○ ○
	TASK ACCOMPLISHED ☐ intimacy level ○ ○ ○ ○ ○

NOTES

....

....

OVERCOMING FEARFUL AVOIDANT ATTACHMENT WORKSHEET

This table will help you examine the impact of the repercussions of the fearful avoidant attachment style on your social interactions on a daily, weekly or monthly basis... The aim of this paper is to develop an appropriate coping plan to control negative signs if you want to bring about real change in your personality.

FEARFUL AVOIDANT ATTACHMENT TAGS AND TRAITS	What are the characteristics of a fearful avoidant attachment style that you experience today? Describe how this affected your dealings.
	👍 WHAT WAS SO COOL: ✋ WHAT WAS WRONG:

AVOIDANT ATTACHMENT WORKSHEET -DBT-

START YOUR DAY MINDFULLY WITH A FEW MINUTES OF MEDITATION OR MINDFULNESS. THIS PRACTICE WILL HELP YOU FEEL CENTERED, ENHANCE SELF-AWARENESS, AND ESTABLISH A POSITIVE MINDSET FOR THE DAY.
TAKE A MOMENT TO REFLECT ON YOUR EMOTIONS AND EMOTIONAL STATE. ASK YOURSELF ABOUT YOUR FEELINGS, THOUGHTS, AND ANY ATTACHMENT-RELATED PATTERNS YOU MIGHT OBSERVE.
EMBRACE POSITIVE AFFIRMATIONS THAT FOSTER TRUST, VULNERABILITY, AND EMOTIONAL CONNECTION. REPEAT PHRASES LIKE 'I AM DESERVING OF LOVE AND CONNECTION,' 'I AM OPEN TO EMOTIONAL INTIMACY,' OR 'I CAN CONFIDE IN OTHERS WITH MY FEELINGS.'

___ : ___

___ : ___

Daily Wins

Mood Tracking ✔

ANGRY	☐
ANNOYED	☐
ANXIOUS	☐
ASHAMED	☐
EMBARRASSING	☐
COURAGEOUS	☐
CALM	☐
CHEERFUL	☐
COLD	☐
CONFUSED	☐
DISCOURAGED	☐
DISTRACTED	☐
EMBARRASSED	☐
EXCITED	☐
FRIENDLY	☐
GUILTY	☐
HAPPY	☐
HOPEFUL	☐
SOLITARY	☐
BELOVED	☐
NERVOUS	☐
OFFENDED	☐
AFRAID	☐
THOUGHTFUL	☐
TIRED OUT	☐
UNCOMFORTABLE	☐
UNCERTAIN	☐

DAILY MOOD CYCLE

Instructions: Think about your day from start to finish. Color the first square to express your feelings each time of the day. Next, write a word that reflects your feelings, and draw in the circle a picture of your face that reflects your feelings at that moment.

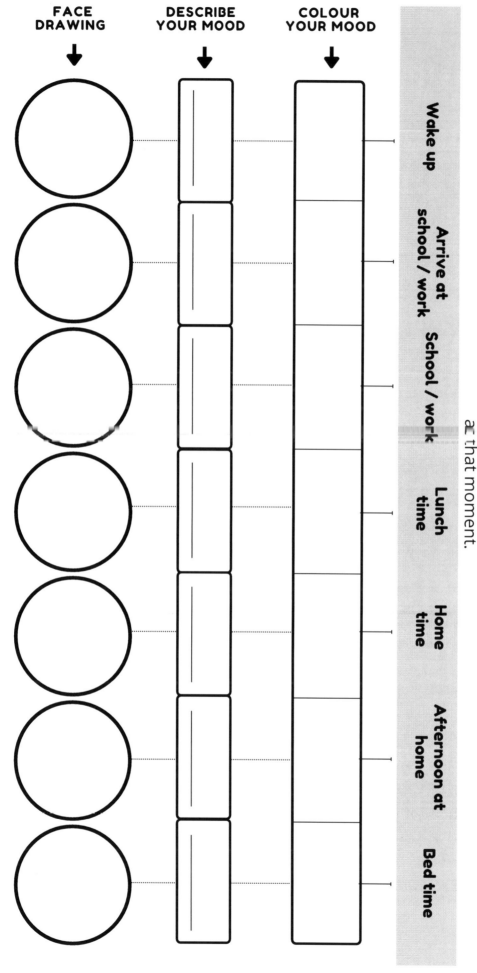

	FACE DRAWING	DESCRIBE YOUR MOOD	COLOUR YOUR MOOD
Wake up			
Arrive at school / work			
School / work			
Lunch time			
Home time			
Afternoon at home			
Bed time			

AVOIDANT ATTACHMENT WORKSHEET

Date : _____

DAILY / WEEKLY - DBT WORKSHEET (OPTIONAL)

- List three emotions that surfaced throughout yesterday. Reflect on how each emotion affected my interactions and decisions.
- Write a kind and supportive message to myself, focusing on self-acceptance and understanding.
- What are the prospects that will make you give up the difficulty of trusting others and open up.
- Write down one boundary I can set today to prioritize my emotional well-being.
- Write down any lingering worries or thoughts before bedtime, and consider ways to ease them.

All about your journey towards changing your negative beliefs about having new romantic relationships.

_____

_____

_____

_____

_____

_____

_____

_____

_____

_____

_____

_____

_____

_____

_____

EXPOSURE THERAPY
FOR
EMOTIONAL CLOSENESS

Individuals with fearful avoidant attachment may struggle to get close to others, feel inferior to themselves and have a negative view of others.

They may avoid emotional intimacy because they see this as a threat. As someone who wants to regain their emotional balance through these exercises, try to engage in low-risk, casual interactions with others. This could mean saying hello to a neighbor or co-worker, or making small talk with a stranger.

About gradually increasing the level of intimacy over time.

	TASK ACCOMPLISHED ☐ intimacy level ○○○○○
	TASK ACCOMPLISHED ☐ intimacy level ○○○○○
	TASK ACCOMPLISHED ☐ intimacy level ○○○○○

NOTES

....

....

OVERCOMING FEARFUL AVOIDANT ATTACHMENT WORKSHEET

This table will help you examine the impact of the repercussions of the fearful avoidant attachment style on your social interactions on a daily, weekly or monthly basis... The aim of this paper is to develop an appropriate coping plan to control negative signs if you want to bring about real change in your personality.

FEARFUL AVOIDANT ATTACHMENT TAGS AND TRAITS	What are the characteristics of a fearful avoidant attachment style that you experience today? Describe how this affected your dealings.
	👍 WHAT WAS SO COOL:
	✋ WHAT WAS WRONG:

AVOIDANT ATTACHMENT WORKSHEET -DBT-

START YOUR DAY MINDFULLY WITH A FEW MINUTES OF MEDITATION OR MINDFULNESS. THIS PRACTICE WILL HELP YOU FEEL CENTERED, ENHANCE SELF-AWARENESS, AND ESTABLISH A POSITIVE MINDSET FOR THE DAY.

TAKE A MOMENT TO REFLECT ON YOUR EMOTIONS AND EMOTIONAL STATE. ASK YOURSELF ABOUT YOUR FEELINGS, THOUGHTS, AND ANY ATTACHMENT-RELATED PATTERNS YOU MIGHT OBSERVE.

EMBRACE POSITIVE AFFIRMATIONS THAT FOSTER TRUST, VULNERABILITY, AND EMOTIONAL CONNECTION. REPEAT PHRASES LIKE "I AM DESERVING OF LOVE AND CONNECTION," "I AM OPEN TO EMOTIONAL INTIMACY," OR "I CAN CONFIDE IN OTHERS WITH MY FEELINGS."

⊘ ___ : ___

⊘ ___ : ___

Mood Tracking

Mood	✓
ANGRY	☐
ANNOYED	☐
ANXIOUS	☐
ASHAMED	☐
EMBARRASSING	☐
COURAGEOUS	☐
CALM	☐
CHEERFUL	☐
COLD	☐
CONFUSED	☐
DISCOURAGED	☐
DISTRACTED	☐
EMBARRASSED	☐
EXCITED	☐
FRIENDLY	☐
GUILTY	☐
HAPPY	☐
HOPEFUL	☐
SOLITARY	☐
BELOVED	☐
NERVOUS	☐
OFFENDED	☐
AFRAID	☐
THOUGHTFUL	☐
TIRED OUT	☐
UNCOMFORTABLE	☐
UNCERTAIN	☐

Daily Wins

DAILY MOOD CYCLE

Instructions: Think about your day from start to finish. Color the first square to express your feelings each time of the day. Next, write a word that reflects your feelings, and draw in the circle a picture of your face that reflects your feelings at that moment.

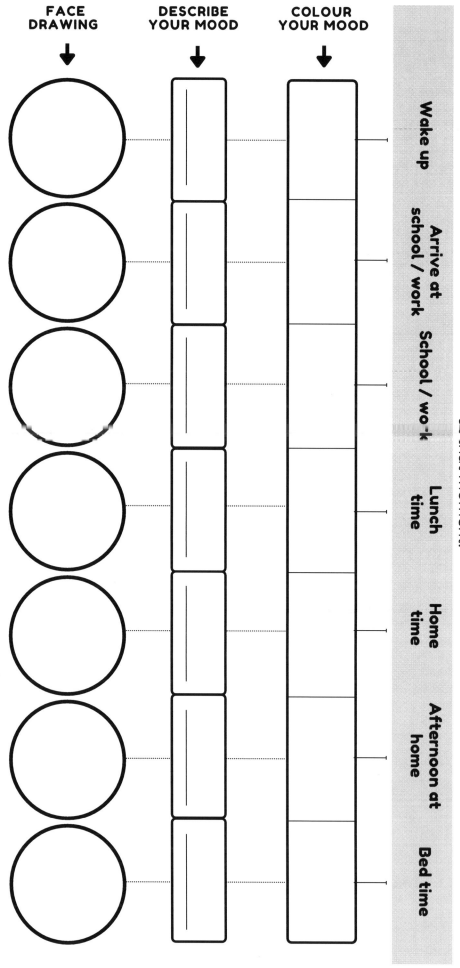

FACE DRAWING

DESCRIBE YOUR MOOD

COLOUR YOUR MOOD

Wake up

Arrive at school / work

School / work

Lunch time

Home time

Afternoon at home

Bed time

AVOIDANT ATTACHMENT WORKSHEET 🔖OPEN

DAILY / WEEKLY - DBT WORKSHEET (OPTIONAL)

- List three emotions that surfaced throughout yesterday. Reflect on how each emotion affected my interactions and decisions.
- Write a kind and supportive message to myself, focusing on self-acceptance and understanding.
- What are the prospects that will make you give up the difficulty of trusting others and open up.
- Write down one boundary I can set today to prioritize my emotional well-being.
- Write down any lingering worries or thoughts before bedtime, and consider ways to ease them.

All about your journey towards changing your negative beliefs about having new romantic relationships.

_____

_____

_____

_____

_____

_____

_____

_____

_____

_____

_____

_____

_____

_____

_____

_____

DATE :   /   /

EXPOSURE THERAPY
FOR
EMOTIONAL CLOSENESS

Individuals with fearful avoidant attachment may struggle to get close to others, feel inferior to themselves and have a negative view of others.

They may avoid emotional intimacy because they see this as a threat. As someone who wants to regain their emotional balance through these exercises, try to engage in low-risk, casual interactions with others. This could mean saying hello to a neighbor or co-worker, or making small talk with a stranger.

About gradually increasing the level of intimacy over time.

	TASK ACCOMPLISHED ☐ intimacy level ○ ○ ○ ○ ○
	TASK ACCOMPLISHED ☐ intimacy level ○ ○ ○ ○ ○
	TASK ACCOMPLISHED ☐ intimacy level ○ ○ ○ ○ ○

NOTES

....

....

OVERCOMING FEARFUL AVOIDANT ATTACHMENT WORKSHEET

This table will help you examine the impact of the repercussions of the fearful avoidant attachment style on your social interactions on a daily, weekly or monthly basis... The aim of this paper is to develop an appropriate coping plan to control negative signs if you want to bring about real change in your personality.

FEARFUL AVOIDANT ATTACHMENT TAGS AND TRAITS	What are the characteristics of a fearful avoidant attachment style that you experience today? Describe how this affected your dealings.
	👍 WHAT WAS SO COOL: ✋ WHAT WAS WRONG:

AVOIDANT ATTACHMENT WORKSHEET -DBT-

Date: / /

Sleep Quality :

START YOUR DAY MINDFULLY WITH A FEW MINUTES OF MEDITATION OR MINDFULNESS. THIS PRACTICE WILL HELP YOU FEEL CENTERED, ENHANCE SELF-AWARENESS, AND ESTABLISH A POSITIVE MINDSET FOR THE DAY.
TAKE A MOMENT TO REFLECT ON YOUR EMOTIONS AND EMOTIONAL STATE. ASK YOURSELF ABOUT YOUR FEELINGS, THOUGHTS, AND ANY ATTACHMENT-RELATED PATTERNS YOU MIGHT OBSERVE.
EMBRACE POSITIVE AFFIRMATIONS THAT FOSTER TRUST, VULNERABILITY, AND EMOTIONAL CONNECTION. REPEAT PHRASES LIKE "I AM DESERVING OF LOVE AND CONNECTION," "I AM OPEN TO EMOTIONAL INTIMACY," OR "I CAN CONFIDE IN OTHERS WITH MY FEELINGS."

___ : ___

___ : ___

Mood Tracking ✓

ANGRY	☐
ANNOYED	☐
ANXIOUS	☐
ASHAMED	☐
EMBARRASSING	☐
COURAGEOUS	☐
CALM	☐
CHEERFUL	☐
COLD	☐
CONFUSED	☐
DISCOURAGED	☐
DISTRACTED	☐
EMBARRASSED	☐
EXCITED	☐
FRIENDLY	☐
GUILTY	☐
HAPPY	☐
HOPEFUL	☐
SOLITARY	☐
BELOVED	☐
NERVOUS	☐
OFFENDED	☐
AFRAID	☐
THOUGHTFUL	☐
TIRED OUT	☐
UNCOMFORTABLE	☐
UNCERTAIN	☐

Daily Wins

DAILY MOOD CYCLE

Instructions: Think about your day from start to finish. Color the first square to express your feelings each time of the day. Next, write a word that reflects your feelings, and draw in the circle a picture of your face that reflects your feelings at that moment.

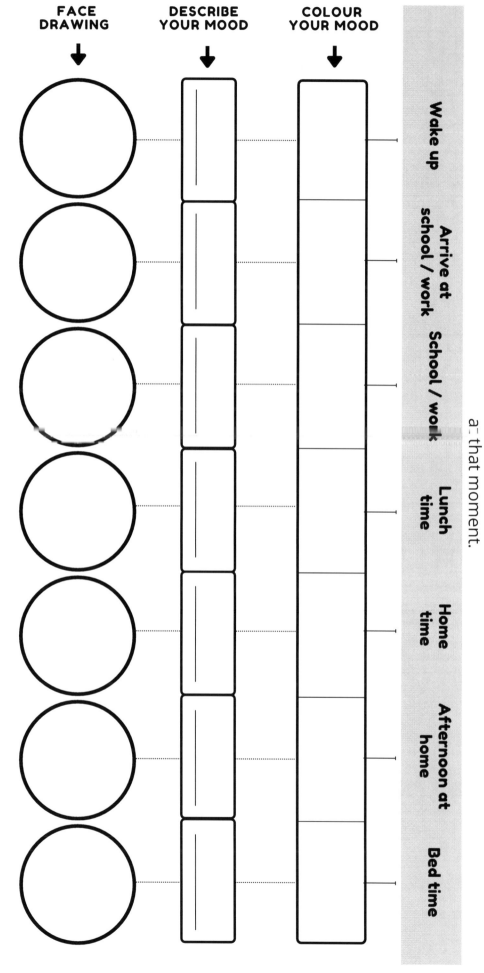

FACE DRAWING

DESCRIBE YOUR MOOD

COLOUR YOUR MOOD

Wake up

Arrive at school / work

School / work

Lunch time

Home time

Afternoon at home

Bed time

AVOIDANT ATTACHMENT WORKSHEET 🪧 OPEN

Date :

- List three emotions that surfaced throughout yesterday. Reflect on how each emotion affected my interactions and decisions.
- Write a kind and supportive message to myself, focusing on self-acceptance and understanding.
- What are the prospects that will make you give up the difficulty of trusting others and open up.
- Write down one boundary I can set today to prioritize my emotional well-being.
- Write down any lingering worries or thoughts before bedtime, and consider ways to ease them.

All about your journey towards changing your negative beliefs about having new romantic relationships.

_____

_____

_____

_____

_____

_____

_____

_____

_____

_____

_____

_____

_____

_____

_____

_____

DATE :   /   /

EXPOSURE THERAPY FOR EMOTIONAL CLOSENESS

Individuals with fearful avoidant attachment may struggle to get close to others, feel inferior to themselves and have a negative view of others.

They may avoid emotional intimacy because they see this as a threat. As someone who wants to regain their emotional balance through these exercises, try to engage in low-risk, casual interactions with others. This could mean saying hello to a neighbor or co-worker, or making small talk with a stranger.

About gradually increasing the level of intimacy over time.

	TASK ACCOMPLISHED □ intimacy level ○ ○ ○ ○ ○
	TASK ACCOMPLISHED □ intimacy level ○ ○ ○ ○ ○
	TASK ACCOMPLISHED □ intimacy level ○ ○ ○ ○ ○

NOTES

....

....

OVERCOMING FEARFUL AVOIDANT ATTACHMENT WORKSHEET

This table will help you examine the impact of the repercussions of the fearful avoidant attachment style on your social interactions on a daily, weekly or monthly basis... The aim of this paper is to develop an appropriate coping plan to control negative signs if you want to bring about real change in your personality.

FEARFUL AVOIDANT ATTACHMENT TAGS AND TRAITS	What are the characteristics of a fearful avoidant attachment style that you experience today? Describe how this affected your dealings.
	👍 WHAT WAS SO COOL: ✋ WHAT WAS WRONG:

AVOIDANT ATTACHMENT WORKSHEET -DBT-

START YOUR DAY MINDFULLY WITH A FEW MINUTES OF MEDITATION OR MINDFULNESS. THIS PRACTICE WILL HELP YOU FEEL CENTERED, ENHANCE SELF-AWARENESS, AND ESTABLISH A POSITIVE MINDSET FOR THE DAY.
TAKE A MOMENT TO REFLECT ON YOUR EMOTIONS AND EMOTIONAL STATE. ASK YOURSELF ABOUT YOUR FEELINGS, THOUGHTS, AND ANY ATTACHMENT-RELATED PATTERNS YOU MIGHT OBSERVE.
EMBRACE POSITIVE AFFIRMATIONS THAT FOSTER TRUST, VULNERABILITY, AND EMOTIONAL CONNECTION. REPEAT PHRASES LIKE 'I AM DESERVING OF LOVE AND CONNECTION,' 'I AM OPEN TO EMOTIONAL INTIMACY,' OR 'I CAN CONFIDE IN OTHERS WITH MY FEELINGS.'

⊘ ___ : ___

⊘ ___ : ___

Daily Wins

Mood Tracking ✓

Mood	
ANGRY	☐
ANNOYED	☐
ANXIOUS	☐
ASHAMED	☐
EMBARRASSING	☐
COURAGEOUS	☐
CALM	☐
CHEERFUL	☐
COLD	☐
CONFUSED	☐
DISCOURAGED	☐
DISTRACTED	☐
EMBARRASSED	☐
EXCITED	☐
FRIENDLY	☐
GUILTY	☐
HAPPY	☐
HOPEFUL	☐
SOLITARY	☐
BELOVED	☐
NERVOUS	☐
OFFENDED	☐
AFRAID	☐
THOUGHTFUL	☐
TIRED OUT	☐
UNCOMFORTABLE	☐
UNCERTAIN	☐

DAILY MOOD CYCLE

Instructions: Think about your day from start to finish. Color the first square to express your feelings each time of the day. Next, write a word that reflects your feelings, and draw in the circle a picture of your face that reflects your feelings at that moment.

FACE DRAWING

DESCRIBE YOUR MOOD

COLOUR YOUR MOOD

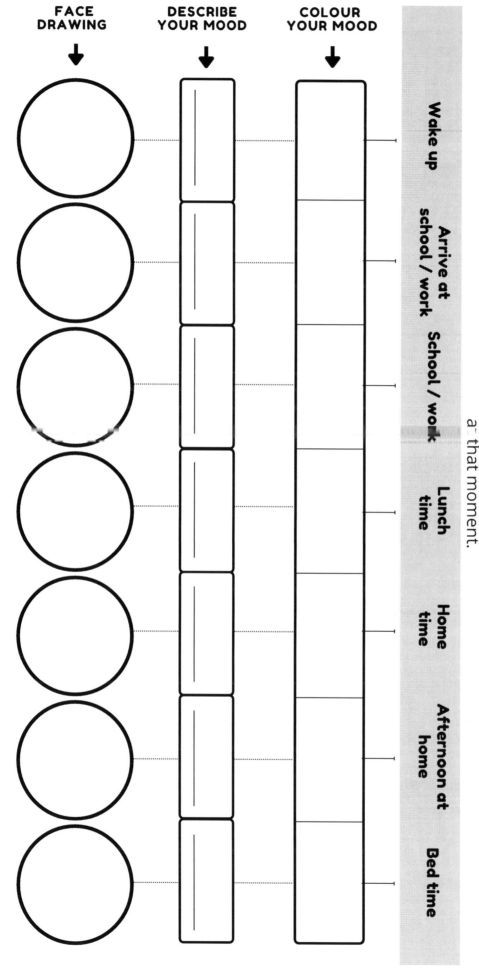

Wake up

Arrive at school / work

School / work

Lunch time

Home time

Afternoon at home

Bed time

AVOIDANT ATTACHMENT WORKSHEET 🪧 OPEN

Date : _____

DAILY / WEEKLY - DBT WORKSHEET (OPTIONAL)

- List three emotions that surfaced throughout yesterday. Reflect on how each emotion affected my interactions and decisions.
- Write a kind and supportive message to myself, focusing on self-acceptance and understanding.
- What are the prospects that will make you give up the difficulty of trusting others and open up.
- Write down one boundary I can set today to prioritize my emotional well-being.
- Write down any lingering worries or thoughts before bedtime, and consider ways to ease them.

All about your journey towards changing your negative beliefs about having new romantic relationships.

EXPOSURE THERAPY
FOR
EMOTIONAL CLOSENESS

Individuals with fearful avoidant attachment may struggle to get close to others, feel inferior to themselves and have a negative view of others.

They may avoid emotional intimacy because they see this as a threat. As someone who wants to regain their emotional balance through these exercises, try to engage in low-risk, casual interactions with others. This could mean saying hello to a neighbor or co-worker, or making small talk with a stranger.

About gradually increasing the level of intimacy over time.

	TASK ACCOMPLISHED ☐ intimacy level ○ ○ ○ ○ ○
	TASK ACCOMPLISHED ☐ intimacy level ○ ○ ○ ○ ○
	TASK ACCOMPLISHED ☐ intimacy level ○ ○ ○ ○ ○

NOTES

....

....

OVERCOMING FEARFUL AVOIDANT ATTACHMENT WORKSHEET

This table will help you examine the impact of the repercussions of the fearful avoidant attachment style on your social interactions on a daily, weekly or monthly basis... The aim of this paper is to develop an appropriate coping plan to control negative signs if you want to bring about real change in your personality.

FEARFUL AVOIDANT ATTACHMENT TAGS AND TRAITS	What are the characteristics of a fearful avoidant attachment style that you experience today? Describe how this affected your dealings.
	👍 WHAT WAS SO COOL:
	✋ WHAT WAS WRONG:

AVOIDANT ATTACHMENT WORKSHEET -DBT-

START YOUR DAY MINDFULLY WITH A FEW MINUTES OF MEDITATION OR MINDFULNESS. THIS PRACTICE WILL HELP YOU FEEL CENTERED, ENHANCE SELF-AWARENESS, AND ESTABLISH A POSITIVE MINDSET FOR THE DAY.
TAKE A MOMENT TO REFLECT ON YOUR EMOTIONS AND EMOTIONAL STATE. ASK YOURSELF ABOUT YOUR FEELINGS, THOUGHTS, AND ANY ATTACHMENT-RELATED PATTERNS YOU MIGHT OBSERVE.
EMBRACE POSITIVE AFFIRMATIONS THAT FOSTER TRUST, VULNERABILITY, AND EMOTIONAL CONNECTION. REPEAT PHRASES LIKE "I AM DESERVING OF LOVE AND CONNECTION," "I AM OPEN TO EMOTIONAL INTIMACY," OR "I CAN CONFIDE IN OTHERS WITH MY FEELINGS."

✓ ___ : ___

✓ ___ : ___

Daily Wins

Mood Tracking ✓

- ANGRY ☐
- ANNOYED ☐
- ANXIOUS ☐
- ASHAMED ☐
- EMBARRASSING ☐
- COURAGEOUS ☐
- CALM ☐
- CHEERFUL ☐
- COLD ☐
- CONFUSED ☐
- DISCOURAGED ☐
- DISTRACTED ☐
- EMBARRASSED ☐
- EXCITED ☐
- FRIENDLY ☐
- GUILTY ☐
- HAPPY ☐
- HOPEFUL ☐
- SOLITARY ☐
- BELOVED ☐
- NERVOUS ☐
- OFFENDED ☐
- AFRAID ☐
- THOUGHTFUL ☐
- TIRED OUT ☐
- UNCOMFORTABLE ☐
- UNCERTAIN ☐

DAILY MOOD CYCLE

Instructions: Think about your day from start to finish. Color the first square to express your feelings each time of the day. Next, write a word that reflects your feelings, and draw in the circle a picture of your face that reflects your feelings at that moment.

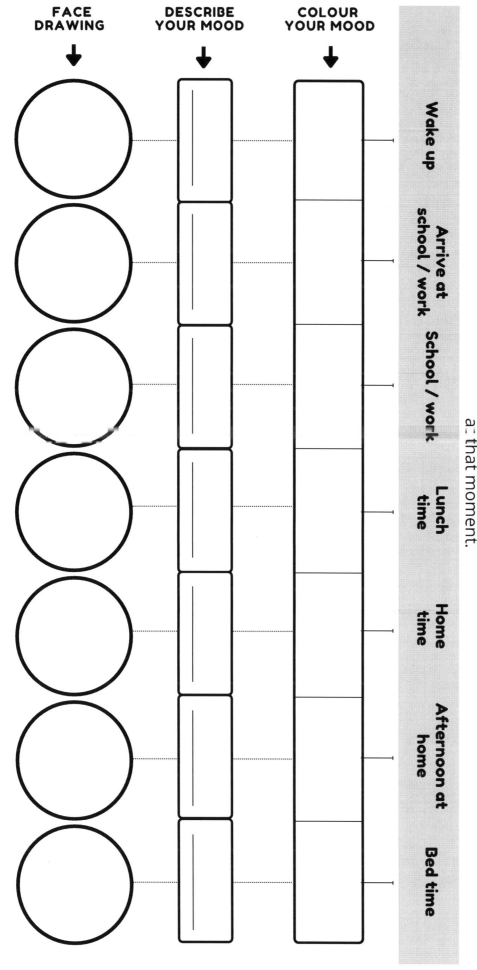

FACE DRAWING

DESCRIBE YOUR MOOD

COLOUR YOUR MOOD

Wake up

Arrive at school / work

School / work

Lunch time

Home time

Afternoon at home

Bed time

AVOIDANT ATTACHMENT WORKSHEET

Date : _____

DAILY / WEEKLY - DBT WORKSHEET (OPTIONAL)

- List three emotions that surfaced throughout yesterday. Reflect on how each emotion affected my interactions and decisions.
- Write a kind and supportive message to myself, focusing on self-acceptance and understanding.
- What are the prospects that will make you give up the difficulty of trusting others and open up.
- Write down one boundary I can set today to prioritize my emotional well-being.
- Write down any lingering worries or thoughts before bedtime, and consider ways to ease them.

All about your journey towards changing your negative beliefs about having new romantic relationships.

_____

_____

_____

_____

_____

_____

_____

_____

_____

_____

_____

_____

_____

_____

_____

DATE :   /   /

EXPOSURE THERAPY
FOR
EMOTIONAL CLOSENESS

Individuals with fearful avoidant attachment may struggle to get close to others, feel inferior to themselves and have a negative view of others.

They may avoid emotional intimacy because they see this as a threat. As someone who wants to regain their emotional balance through these exercises, try to engage in low-risk, casual interactions with others. This could mean saying hello to a neighbor or co-worker, or making small talk with a stranger.

About gradually increasing the level of intimacy over time.

	TASK ACCOMPLISHED ☐ intimacy level ○ ○ ○ ○ ○
	TASK ACCOMPLISHED ☐ intimacy level ○ ○ ○ ○ ○
	TASK ACCOMPLISHED ☐ intimacy level ○ ○ ○ ○ ○

NOTES

....

....

OVERCOMING FEARFUL AVOIDANT ATTACHMENT WORKSHEET

This table will help you examine the impact of the repercussions of the fearful avoidant attachment style on your social interactions on a daily, weekly or monthly basis... The aim of this paper is to develop an appropriate coping plan to control negative signs if you want to bring about real change in your personality.

FEARFUL AVOIDANT ATTACHMENT TAGS AND TRAITS	What are the characteristics of a fearful avoidant attachment style that you experience today? Describe how this affected your dealings.
	👍 WHAT WAS SO COOL· ✋ WHAT WAS WRONG:

AVOIDANT ATTACHMENT WORKSHEET -DBT-

START YOUR DAY MINDFULLY WITH A FEW MINUTES OF MEDITATION OR MINDFULNESS. THIS PRACTICE WILL HELP YOU FEEL CENTERED, ENHANCE SELF-AWARENESS, AND ESTABLISH A POSITIVE MINDSET FOR THE DAY.
TAKE A MOMENT TO REFLECT ON YOUR EMOTIONS AND EMOTIONAL STATE. ASK YOURSELF ABOUT YOUR FEELINGS, THOUGHTS, AND ANY ATTACHMENT-RELATED PATTERNS YOU MIGHT OBSERVE.
EMBRACE POSITIVE AFFIRMATIONS THAT FOSTER TRUST, VULNERABILITY, AND EMOTIONAL CONNECTION. REPEAT PHRASES LIKE "I AM DESERVING OF LOVE AND CONNECTION," "I AM OPEN TO EMOTIONAL INTIMACY," OR "I CAN CONFIDE IN OTHERS WITH MY FEELINGS."

✓ ___ : ___

_____

_____

_____

✓ ___ : ___

_____

_____

_____

Mood Tracking

Mood	
ANGRY	☐
ANNOYED	☐
ANXIOUS	☐
ASHAMED	☐
EMBARRASSING	☐
COURAGEOUS	☐
CALM	☐
CHEERFUL	☐
COLD	☐
CONFUSED	☐
DISCOURAGED	☐
DISTRACTED	☐
EMBARRASSED	☐
EXCITED	☐
FRIENDLY	☐
GUILTY	☐
HAPPY	☐
HOPEFUL	☐
SOLITARY	☐
BELOVED	☐
NERVOUS	☐
OFFENDED	☐
AFRAID	☐
THOUGHTFUL	☐
TIRED OUT	☐
UNCOMFORTABLE	☐
UNCERTAIN	☐

Daily Wins

_____

_____

_____

DAILY MOOD CYCLE

Instructions: Think about your day from start to finish. Color the first square to express your feelings each time of the day. Next, write a word that reflects your feelings, and draw in the circle a picture of your face that reflects your feelings at that moment.

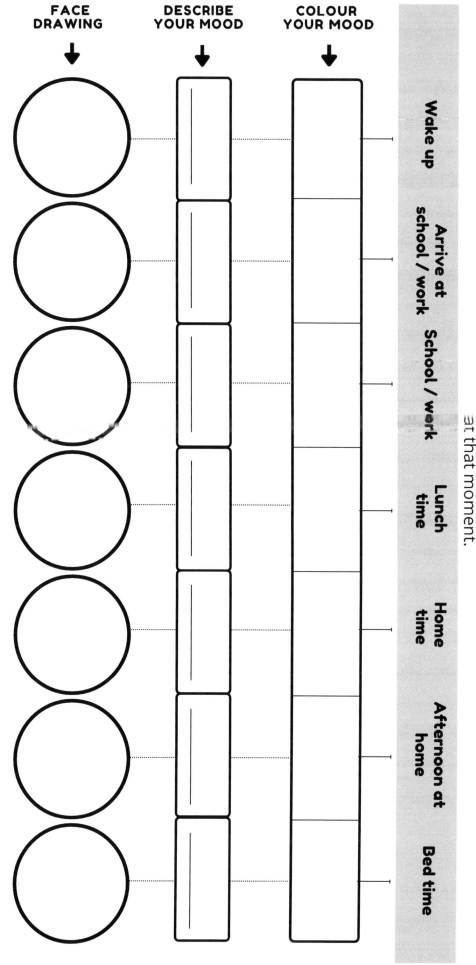

FACE DRAWING

DESCRIBE YOUR MOOD

COLOUR YOUR MOOD

- Wake up
- Arrive at school / work
- School / work
- Lunch time
- Home time
- Afternoon at home
- Bed time

AVOIDANT ATTACHMENT WORKSHEET

OPEN

Date : _____

DAILY / WEEKLY - DBT WORKSHEET (OPTIONAL)

- List three emotions that surfaced throughout yesterday. Reflect on how each emotion affected my interactions and decisions.
- Write a kind and supportive message to myself, focusing on self-acceptance and understanding.
- What are the prospects that will make you give up the difficulty of trusting others and open up.
- Write down one boundary I can set today to prioritize my emotional well-being.
- Write down any lingering worries or thoughts before bedtime, and consider ways to ease them.

All about your journey towards changing your negative beliefs about having new romantic relationships.

_____

_____

_____

_____

_____

_____

_____

_____

_____

_____

_____

_____

_____

_____

_____

DATE :   /   /

EXPOSURE THERAPY FOR EMOTIONAL CLOSENESS

Individuals with fearful avoidant attachment may struggle to get close to others, feel inferior to themselves and have a negative view of others.

They may avoid emotional intimacy because they see this as a threat. As someone who wants to regain their emotional balance through these exercises, try to engage in low-risk, casual interactions with others. This could mean saying hello to a neighbor or co-worker, or making small talk with a stranger.

About gradually increasing the level of intimacy over time.

	TASK ACCOMPLISHED ☐ intimacy level ○○○○○
	TASK ACCOMPLISHED ☐ intimacy level ○○○○○
	TASK ACCOMPLISHED ☐ intimacy level ○○○○○

NOTES

....

....

OVERCOMING FEARFUL AVOIDANT ATTACHMENT WORKSHEET

This table will help you examine the impact of the repercussions of the fearful avoidant attachment style on your social interactions on a daily, weekly or monthly basis... The aim of this paper is to develop an appropriate coping plan to control negative signs if you want to bring about real change in your personality.

FEARFUL AVOIDANT ATTACHMENT TAGS AND TRAITS	What are the characteristics of a fearful avoidant attachment style that you experience today? Describe how this affected your dealings.
	👉 WHAT WAS SO COOL.
	✋ WHAT WAS WRONG:

AVOIDANT ATTACHMENT WORKSHEET -DBT-

START YOUR DAY MINDFULLY WITH A FEW MINUTES OF MEDITATION OR MINDFULNESS. THIS PRACTICE WILL HELP YOU FEEL CENTERED, ENHANCE SELF-AWARENESS, AND ESTABLISH A POSITIVE MINDSET FOR THE DAY.
TAKE A MOMENT TO REFLECT ON YOUR EMOTIONS AND EMOTIONAL STATE. ASK YOURSELF ABOUT YOUR FEELINGS, THOUGHTS, AND ANY ATTACHMENT-RELATED PATTERNS YOU MIGHT OBSERVE.
EMBRACE POSITIVE AFFIRMATIONS THAT FOSTER TRUST, VULNERABILITY, AND EMOTIONAL CONNECTION. REPEAT PHRASES LIKE "I AM DESERVING OF LOVE AND CONNECTION," "I AM OPEN TO EMOTIONAL INTIMACY," OR "I CAN CONFIDE IN OTHERS WITH MY FEELINGS."

✓ ___ : ___

_____
_____
_____
_____

✓ ___ : ___

_____
_____
_____
_____

Daily Wins

_____
_____
_____

Mood Tracking

ANGRY	☐
ANNOYED	☐
ANXIOUS	☐
ASHAMED	☐
EMBARRASSING	☐
COURAGEOUS	☐
CALM	☐
CHEERFUL	☐
COLD	☐
CONFUSED	☐
DISCOURAGED	☐
DISTRACTED	☐
EMBARRASSED	☐
EXCITED	☐
FRIENDLY	☐
GUILTY	☐
HAPPY	☐
HOPEFUL	☐
SOLITARY	☐
BELOVED	☐
NERVOUS	☐
OFFENDED	☐
AFRAID	☐
THOUGHTFUL	☐
TIRED OUT	☐
UNCOMFORTABLE	☐
UNCERTAIN	☐

DAILY MOOD CYCLE

Instructions: Think about your day from start to finish. Color the first square to express your feelings each time of the day. Next, write a word that reflects your feelings, and draw in the circle a picture of your face that reflects your feelings at that moment.

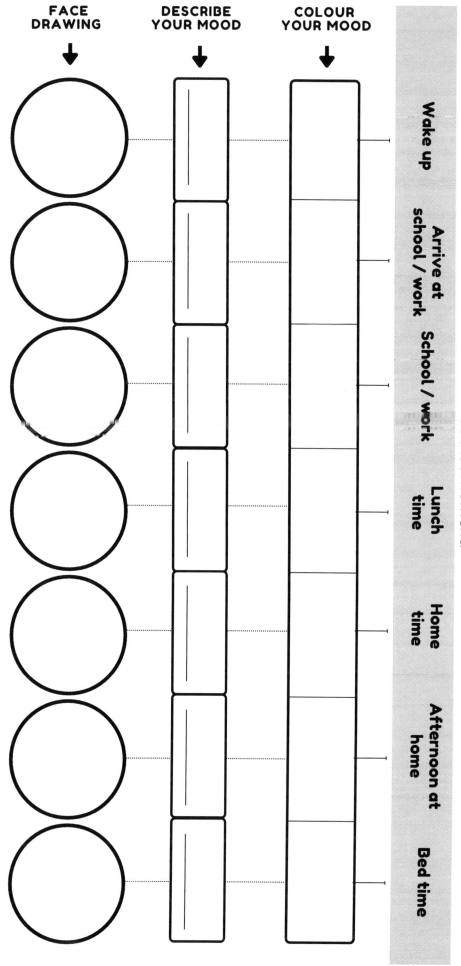

FACE DRAWING

DESCRIBE YOUR MOOD

COLOUR YOUR MOOD

Wake up

Arrive at school / work

School / work

Lunch time

Home time

Afternoon at home

Bed time

AVOIDANT ATTACHMENT WORKSHEET

Date : _____

DAILY / WEEKLY - DBT WORKSHEET (OPTIONAL)

- List three emotions that surfaced throughout yesterday. Reflect on how each emotion affected my interactions and decisions.
- Write a kind and supportive message to myself, focusing on self-acceptance and understanding.
- What are the prospects that will make you give up the difficulty of trusting others and open up.
- Write down one boundary I can set today to prioritize my emotional well-being.
- Write down any lingering worries or thoughts before bedtime, and consider ways to ease them.

All about your journey towards changing your negative beliefs about having new romantic relationships.

_____

_____

_____

_____

_____

_____

_____

_____

_____

_____

_____

_____

_____

_____

_____

DATE :   /   /

EXPOSURE THERAPY
FOR
EMOTIONAL CLOSENESS

Individuals with fearful avoidant attachment may struggle to get close to others, feel inferior to themselves and have a negative view of others.

They may avoid emotional intimacy because they see this as a threat. As someone who wants to regain their emotional balance through these exercises, try to engage in low-risk, casual interactions with others. This could mean saying hello to a neighbor or co-worker, or making small talk with a stranger.

About gradually increasing the level of intimacy over time.

	TASK ACCOMPLISHED □
	intimacy level ○ ○ ○ ○ ○
	TASK ACCOMPLISHED □
	intimacy level ○ ○ ○ ○ ○
	TASK ACCOMPLISHED □
	intimacy level ○ ○ ○ ○ ○

NOTES

....

....

OVERCOMING FEARFUL AVOIDANT ATTACHMENT WORKSHEET

This table will help you examine the impact of the repercussions of the fearful avoidant attachment style on your social interactions on a daily, weekly or monthly basis... The aim of this paper is to develop an appropriate coping plan to control negative signs if you want to bring about real change in your personality.

FEARFUL AVOIDANT ATTACHMENT TAGS AND TRAITS	What are the characteristics of a fearful avoidant attachment style that you experience today? Describe how this affected your dealings.
	👍 WHAT WAS SO COOL: ✋ WHAT WAS WRONG:

AVOIDANT ATTACHMENT WORKSHEET -DBT-

START YOUR DAY MINDFULLY WITH A FEW MINUTES OF MEDITATION OR MINDFULNESS. THIS PRACTICE WILL HELP YOU FEEL CENTERED, ENHANCE SELF-AWARENESS, AND ESTABLISH A POSITIVE MINDSET FOR THE DAY.
TAKE A MOMENT TO REFLECT ON YOUR EMOTIONS AND EMOTIONAL STATE. ASK YOURSELF ABOUT YOUR FEELINGS, THOUGHTS, AND ANY ATTACHMENT-RELATED PATTERNS YOU MIGHT OBSERVE.
EMBRACE POSITIVE AFFIRMATIONS THAT FOSTER TRUST, VULNERABILITY, AND EMOTIONAL CONNECTION. REPEAT PHRASES LIKE "I AM DESERVING OF LOVE AND CONNECTION," "I AM OPEN TO EMOTIONAL INTIMACY," OR "I CAN CONFIDE IN OTHERS WITH MY FEELINGS."

✓ ___ : ___

✓ ___ : ___

Mood Tracking

- ANGRY ☐
- ANNOYED ☐
- ANXIOUS ☐
- ASHAMED ☐
- EMBARRASSING ☐
- COURAGEOUS ☐
- CALM ☐
- CHEERFUL ☐
- COLD ☐
- CONFUSED ☐
- DISCOURAGED ☐
- DISTRACTED ☐
- EMBARRASSED ☐
- EXCITED ☐
- FRIENDLY ☐
- GUILTY ☐
- HAPPY ☐
- HOPEFUL ☐
- SOLITARY ☐
- BELOVED ☐
- NERVOUS ☐
- OFFENDED ☐
- AFRAID ☐
- THOUGHTFUL ☐
- TIRED OUT ☐
- UNCOMFORTABLE ☐
- UNCERTAIN ☐

Daily Wins

DAILY MOOD CYCLE

Instructions: Think about your day from start to finish. Color the first square to express your feelings each time of the day. Next, write a word that reflects your feelings, and draw in the circle a picture of your face that reflects your feelings at that moment.

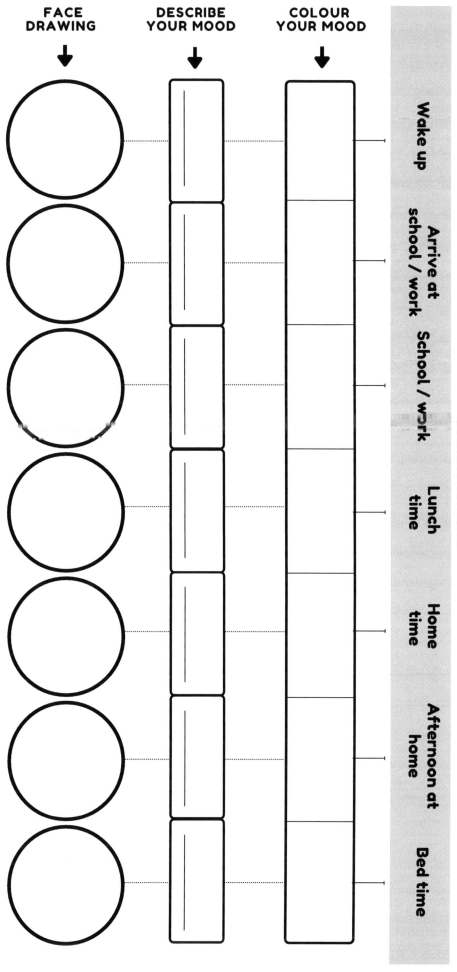

FACE DRAWING

DESCRIBE YOUR MOOD

COLOUR YOUR MOOD

Wake up

Arrive at school / work

School / work

Lunch time

Home time

Afternoon at home

Bed time

AVOIDANT ATTACHMENT WORKSHEET OPEN

Date : _____

DAILY / WEEKLY - DBT WORKSHEET (OPTIONAL)

- List three emotions that surfaced throughout yesterday. Reflect on how each emotion affected my interactions and decisions.
- Write a kind and supportive message to myself, focusing on self-acceptance and understanding.
- What are the prospects that will make you give up the difficulty of trusting others and open up.
- Write down one boundary I can set today to prioritize my emotional well-being.
- Write down any lingering worries or thoughts before bedtime, and consider ways to ease them.

All about your journey towards changing your negative beliefs about having new romantic relationships.

_____

_____

_____

_____

_____

_____

_____

_____

_____

_____

_____

_____

_____

_____

_____

DATE :   /   /

EXPOSURE THERAPY
FOR
EMOTIONAL CLOSENESS

Individuals with fearful avoidant attachment may struggle to get close to others, feel inferior to themselves and have a negative view of others.

They may avoid emotional intimacy because they see this as a threat. As someone who wants to regain their emotional balance through these exercises, try to engage in low-risk, casual interactions with others. This could mean saying hello to a neighbor or co-worker, or making small talk with a stranger.

About gradually increasing the level of intimacy over time.

	TASK ACCOMPLISHED ☐ intimacy level ○ ○ ○ ○ ○
	TASK ACCOMPLISHED ☐ intimacy level ○ ○ ○ ○ ○
	TASK ACCOMPLISHED ☐ intimacy level ○ ○ ○ ○ ○

NOTES

....

....

OVERCOMING FEARFUL AVOIDANT ATTACHMENT WORKSHEET

This table will help you examine the impact of the repercussions of the fearful avoidant attachment style on your social interactions on a daily, weekly or monthly basis... The aim of this paper is to develop an appropriate coping plan to control negative signs if you want to bring about real change in your personality.

FEARFUL AVOIDANT ATTACHMENT TAGS AND TRAITS	What are the characteristics of a fearful avoidant attachment style that you experience today? Describe how this affected your dealings.
	👍 WHAT WAS SO COOL. ✋ WHAT WAS WRONG:

AVOIDANT ATTACHMENT WORKSHEET -DBT-

START YOUR DAY MINDFULLY WITH A FEW MINUTES OF MEDITATION OR MINDFULNESS. THIS PRACTICE WILL HELP YOU FEEL CENTERED, ENHANCE SELF-AWARENESS, AND ESTABLISH A POSITIVE MINDSET FOR THE DAY.
TAKE A MOMENT TO REFLECT ON YOUR EMOTIONS AND EMOTIONAL STATE. ASK YOURSELF ABOUT YOUR FEELINGS, THOUGHTS, AND ANY ATTACHMENT-RELATED PATTERNS YOU MIGHT OBSERVE.
EMBRACE POSITIVE AFFIRMATIONS THAT FOSTER TRUST, VULNERABILITY, AND EMOTIONAL CONNECTION. REPEAT PHRASES LIKE "I AM DESERVING OF LOVE AND CONNECTION," "I AM OPEN TO EMOTIONAL INTIMACY," OR "I CAN CONFIDE IN OTHERS WITH MY FEELINGS."

✓ ___ : ___

✓ ___ : ___

Daily Wins

Mood Tracking ✔

ANGRY	☐
ANNOYED	☐
ANXIOUS	☐
ASHAMED	☐
EMBARRASSING	☐
COURAGEOUS	☐
CALM	☐
CHEERFUL	☐
COLD	☐
CONFUSED	☐
DISCOURAGED	☐
DISTRACTED	☐
EMBARRASSED	☐
EXCITED	☐
FRIENDLY	☐
GUILTY	☐
HAPPY	☐
HOPEFUL	☐
SOLITARY	☐
BELOVED	☐
NERVOUS	☐
OFFENDED	☐
AFRAID	☐
THOUGHTFUL	☐
TIRED OUT	☐
UNCOMFORTABLE	☐
UNCERTAIN	☐

DAILY MOOD CYCLE

Instructions: Think about your day from start to finish. Color the first square to express your feelings each time of the day. Next, write a word that reflects your feelings, and draw in the circle a picture of your face that reflects your feelings at that moment.

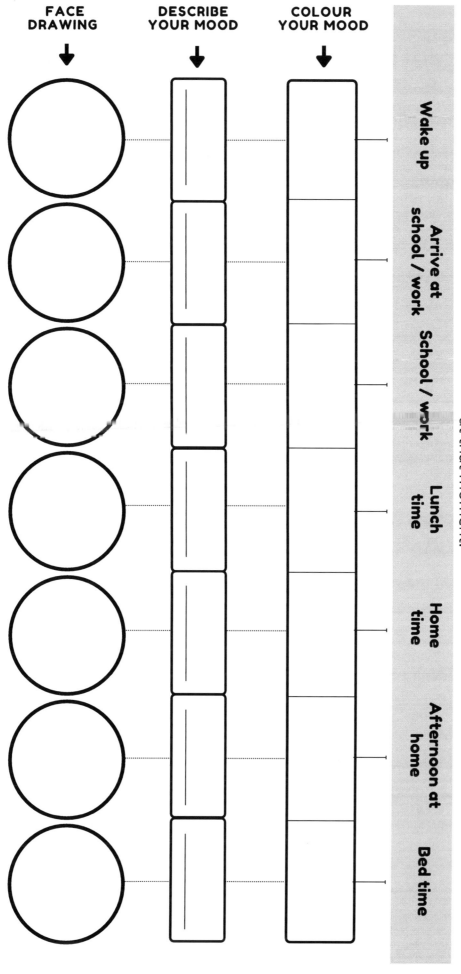

FACE DRAWING

DESCRIBE YOUR MOOD

COLOUR YOUR MOOD

Wake up

Arrive at school / work

School / work

Lunch time

Home time

Afternoon at home

Bed time

AVOIDANT ATTACHMENT WORKSHEET

Date : _____

DAILY / WEEKLY - DBT WORKSHEET (OPTIONAL)

- List three emotions that surfaced throughout yesterday. Reflect on how each emotion affected my interactions and decisions.
- Write a kind and supportive message to myself, focusing on self-acceptance and understanding.
- What are the prospects that will make you give up the difficulty of trusting others and open up.
- Write down one boundary I can set today to prioritize my emotional well-being.
- Write down any lingering worries or thoughts before bedtime, and consider ways to ease them.

All about your journey towards changing your negative beliefs about having new romantic relationships.

_____

_____

_____

_____

_____

_____

_____

_____

_____

_____

_____

_____

_____

_____

_____

_____

_____

EXPOSURE THERAPY
FOR
EMOTIONAL CLOSENESS

Individuals with fearful avoidant attachment may struggle to get close to others, feel inferior to themselves and have a negative view of others.

They may avoid emotional intimacy because they see this as a threat. As someone who wants to regain their emotional balance through these exercises, try to engage in low-risk, casual interactions with others. This could mean saying hello to a neighbor or co-worker, or making small talk with a stranger.
About gradually increasing the level of intimacy over time.

	TASK ACCOMPLISHED ☐ intimacy level ◯ ◯ ◯ ◯ ◯
	TASK ACCOMPLISHED ☐ intimacy level ◯ ◯ ◯ ◯ ◯
	TASK ACCOMPLISHED ☐ intimacy level ◯ ◯ ◯ ◯ ◯

NOTES

....

....

OVERCOMING FEARFUL AVOIDANT ATTACHMENT WORKSHEET

This table will help you examine the impact of the repercussions of the fearful avoidant attachment style on your social interactions on a daily, weekly or monthly basis... The aim of this paper is to develop an appropriate coping plan to control negative signs if you want to bring about real change in your personality.

FEARFUL AVOIDANT ATTACHMENT TAGS AND TRAITS	What are the characteristics of a fearful avoidant attachment style that you experience today? Describe how this affected your dealings.
	👍 WHAT WAS SO COOL! ✋ WHAT WAS WRONG:

AVOIDANT ATTACHMENT WORKSHEET -DBT-

START YOUR DAY MINDFULLY WITH A FEW MINUTES OF MEDITATION OR MINDFULNESS. THIS PRACTICE WILL HELP YOU FEEL CENTERED, ENHANCE SELF-AWARENESS, AND ESTABLISH A POSITIVE MINDSET FOR THE DAY.
TAKE A MOMENT TO REFLECT ON YOUR EMOTIONS AND EMOTIONAL STATE. ASK YOURSELF ABOUT YOUR FEELINGS, THOUGHTS, AND ANY ATTACHMENT-RELATED PATTERNS YOU MIGHT OBSERVE.
EMBRACE POSITIVE AFFIRMATIONS THAT FOSTER TRUST, VULNERABILITY, AND EMOTIONAL CONNECTION. REPEAT PHRASES LIKE "I AM DESERVING OF LOVE AND CONNECTION," "I AM OPEN TO EMOTIONAL INTIMACY," OR "I CAN CONFIDE IN OTHERS WITH MY FEELINGS."

$\checkmark$ ___ : ___

_____

_____

_____

$\checkmark$ ___ : ___

_____

_____

_____

Daily Wins

_____

_____

_____

Date: / /

Sleep Quality :

Mood Tracking ✓

ANGRY	☐
ANNOYED	☐
ANXIOUS	☐
ASHAMED	☐
EMBARRASSING	☐
COURAGEOUS	☐
CALM	☐
CHEERFUL	☐
COLD	☐
CONFUSED	☐
DISCOURAGED	☐
DISTRACTED	☐
EMBARRASSED	☐
EXCITED	☐
FRIENDLY	☐
GUILTY	☐
HAPPY	☐
HOPEFUL	☐
SOLITARY	☐
BELOVED	☐
NERVOUS	☐
OFFENDED	☐
AFRAID	☐
THOUGHTFUL	☐
TIRED OUT	☐
UNCOMFORTABLE	☐
UNCERTAIN	☐

DAILY MOOD CYCLE

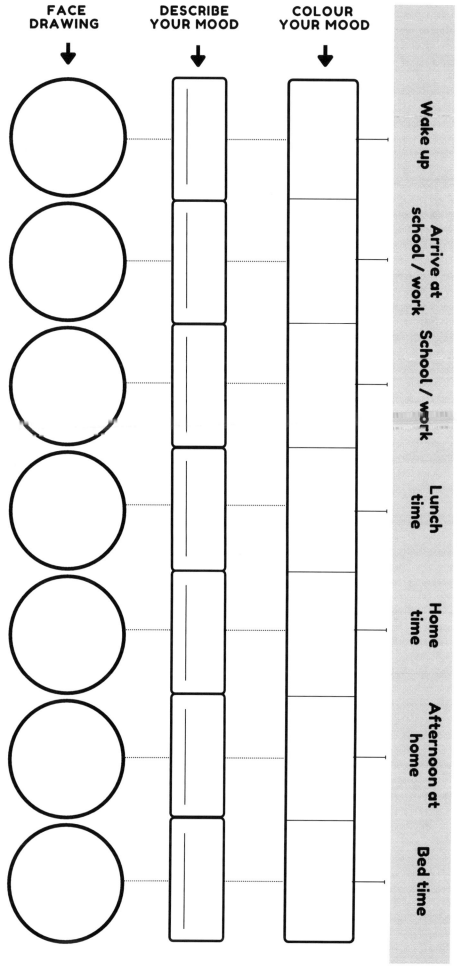

FACE DRAWING

DESCRIBE YOUR MOOD

COLOUR YOUR MOOD

Instructions: Think about your day from start to finish. Color the first square to express your feelings each time of the day. Next, write a word that reflects your feelings, and draw in the circle a picture of your face that reflects your feelings at that moment.

Wake up

Arrive at school / work

School / work

Lunch time

Home time

Afternoon at home

Bed time

AVOIDANT ATTACHMENT WORKSHEET 🚪OPEN

Date : _____

DAILY / WEEKLY - DBT WORKSHEET (OPTIONAL)

- List three emotions that surfaced throughout yesterday. Reflect on how each emotion affected my interactions and decisions.
- Write a kind and supportive message to myself, focusing on self-acceptance and understanding.
- What are the prospects that will make you give up the difficulty of trusting others and open up.
- Write down one boundary I can set today to prioritize my emotional well-being.
- Write down any lingering worries or thoughts before bedtime, and consider ways to ease them.

All about your journey towards changing your negative beliefs about having new romantic relationships.

_____

_____

_____

_____

_____

_____

_____

_____

_____

_____

_____

_____

_____

_____

_____

_____

DATE :   /   /

EXPOSURE THERAPY FOR EMOTIONAL CLOSENESS

Individuals with fearful avoidant attachment may struggle to get close to others, feel inferior to themselves and have a negative view of others.

They may avoid emotional intimacy because they see this as a threat. As someone who wants to regain their emotional balance through these exercises, try to engage in low-risk, casual interactions with others. This could mean saying hello to a neighbor or co-worker, or making small talk with a stranger.

About gradually increasing the level of intimacy over time.

	TASK ACCOMPLISHED ☐ intimacy level ○ ○ ○ ○ ○
	TASK ACCOMPLISHED ☐ intimacy level ○ ○ ○ ○ ○
	TASK ACCOMPLISHED ☐ intimacy level ○ ○ ○ ○ ○

NOTES

....

....

OVERCOMING FEARFUL AVOIDANT ATTACHMENT WORKSHEET

This table will help you examine the impact of the repercussions of the fearful avoidant attachment style on your social interactions on a daily, weekly or monthly basis... The aim of this paper is to develop an appropriate coping plan to control negative signs if you want to bring about real change in your personality.

FEARFUL AVOIDANT ATTACHMENT TAGS AND TRAITS	What are the characteristics of a fearful avoidant attachment style that you experience today? Describe how this affected your dealings.
	👍 WIIAT WAO OO COOL: ✋ WHAT WAS WRONG:

AVOIDANT ATTACHMENT WORKSHEET -DBT-

START YOUR DAY MINDFULLY WITH A FEW MINUTES OF MEDITATION OR MINDFULNESS. THIS PRACTICE WILL HELP YOU FEEL CENTERED, ENHANCE SELF-AWARENESS, AND ESTABLISH A POSITIVE MINDSET FOR THE DAY.
TAKE A MOMENT TO REFLECT ON YOUR EMOTIONS AND EMOTIONAL STATE. ASK YOURSELF ABOUT YOUR FEELINGS, THOUGHTS, AND ANY ATTACHMENT-RELATED PATTERNS YOU MIGHT OBSERVE.
EMBRACE POSITIVE AFFIRMATIONS THAT FOSTER TRUST, VULNERABILITY, AND EMOTIONAL CONNECTION. REPEAT PHRASES LIKE "I AM DESERVING OF LOVE AND CONNECTION," "I AM OPEN TO EMOTIONAL INTIMACY," OR "I CAN CONFIDE IN OTHERS WITH MY FEELINGS."

⊘ ___ : ___

⊘ ___ : ___

Daily Wins

Mood Tracking ✓

- ANGRY ☐
- ANNOYED ☐
- ANXIOUS ☐
- ASHAMED ☐
- EMBARRASSING ☐
- COURAGEOUS ☐
- CALM ☐
- CHEERFUL ☐
- COLD ☐
- CONFUSED ☐
- DISCOURAGED ☐
- DISTRACTED ☐
- EMBARRASSED ☐
- EXCITED ☐
- FRIENDLY ☐
- GUILTY ☐
- HAPPY ☐
- HOPEFUL ☐
- SOLITARY ☐
- BELOVED ☐
- NERVOUS ☐
- OFFENDED ☐
- AFRAID ☐
- THOUGHTFUL ☐
- TIRED OUT ☐
- UNCOMFORTABLE ☐
- UNCERTAIN ☐

DAILY MOOD CYCLE

Instructions: Think about your day from start to finish. Color the first square to express your feelings each time of the day. Next, write a word that reflects your feelings, and draw in the circle a picture of your face that reflects your feelings at that moment.

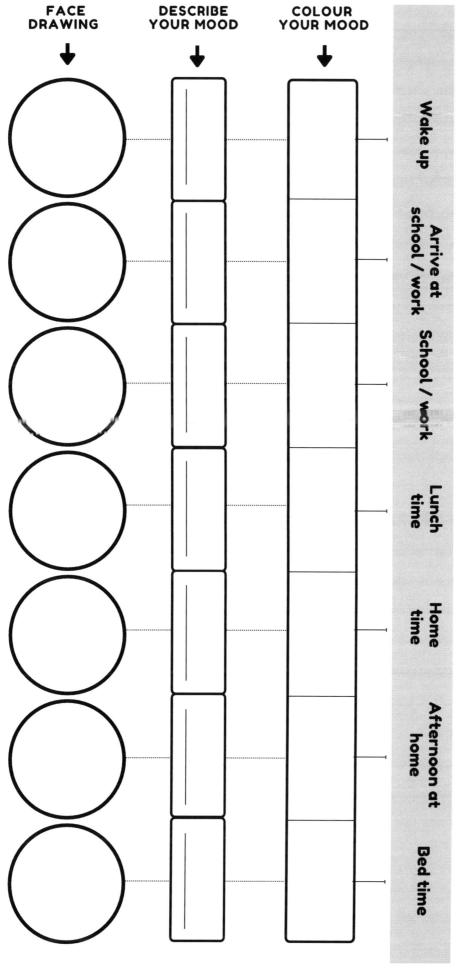

FACE DRAWING

DESCRIBE YOUR MOOD

COLOUR YOUR MOOD

- Wake up
- Arrive at school / work
- School / work
- Lunch time
- Home time
- Afternoon at home
- Bed time

AVOIDANT ATTACHMENT WORKSHEET

Date : _____

DAILY / WEEKLY - DBT WORKSHEET (OPTIONAL)

- List three emotions that surfaced throughout yesterday. Reflect on how each emotion affected my interactions and decisions.
- Write a kind and supportive message to myself, focusing on self-acceptance and understanding.
- What are the prospects that will make you give up the difficulty of trusting others and open up.
- Write down one boundary I can set today to prioritize my emotional well-being.
- Write down any lingering worries or thoughts before bedtime, and consider ways to ease them.

All about your journey towards changing your negative beliefs about having new romantic relationships.

_____

_____

_____

_____

_____

_____

_____

_____

_____

_____

_____

_____

_____

_____

DATE :   /   /

EXPOSURE THERAPY
FOR
EMOTIONAL CLOSENESS

Individuals with fearful avoidant attachment may struggle to get close to others, feel inferior to themselves and have a negative view of others.

They may avoid emotional intimacy because they see this as a threat. As someone who wants to regain their emotional balance through these exercises, try to engage in low-risk, casual interactions with others. This could mean saying hello to a neighbor or co-worker, or making small talk with a stranger.

About gradually increasing the level of intimacy over time.

	TASK ACCOMPLISHED ☐ intimacy level ○ ○ ○ ○ ○
	TASK ACCOMPLISHED ☐ intimacy level ○ ○ ○ ○ ○
	TASK ACCOMPLISHED ☐ intimacy level ○ ○ ○ ○ ○

NOTES

....

....

OVERCOMING FEARFUL AVOIDANT ATTACHMENT WORKSHEET

This table will help you examine the impact of the repercussions of the fearful avoidant attachment style on your social interactions on a daily, weekly or monthly basis... The aim of this paper is to develop an appropriate coping plan to control negative signs if you want to bring about real change in your personality.

FEARFUL AVOIDANT ATTACHMENT TAGS AND TRAITS	What are the characteristics of a fearful avoidant attachment style that you experience today? Describe how this affected your dealings.
	👍 WHAT WAS SO COOL: ✋ WHAT WAS WRONG:

AVOIDANT ATTACHMENT WORKSHEET -DBT-

START YOUR DAY MINDFULLY WITH A FEW MINUTES OF MEDITATION OR MINDFULNESS. THIS PRACTICE WILL HELP YOU FEEL CENTERED, ENHANCE SELF-AWARENESS, AND ESTABLISH A POSITIVE MINDSET FOR THE DAY.

TAKE A MOMENT TO REFLECT ON YOUR EMOTIONS AND EMOTIONAL STATE. ASK YOURSELF ABOUT YOUR FEELINGS, THOUGHTS, AND ANY ATTACHMENT-RELATED PATTERNS YOU MIGHT OBSERVE.

EMBRACE POSITIVE AFFIRMATIONS THAT FOSTER TRUST, VULNERABILITY, AND EMOTIONAL CONNECTION. REPEAT PHRASES LIKE 'I AM DESERVING OF LOVE AND CONNECTION,' 'I AM OPEN TO EMOTIONAL INTIMACY,' OR 'I CAN CONFIDE IN OTHERS WITH MY FEELINGS.'

✓ ___ : ___

✓ ___ : ___

Mood Tracking ✓

- ANGRY ☐
- ANNOYED ☐
- ANXIOUS ☐
- ASHAMED ☐
- EMBARRASSING ☐
- COURAGEOUS ☐
- CALM ☐
- CHEERFUL ☐
- COLD ☐
- CONFUSED ☐
- DISCOURAGED ☐
- DISTRACTED ☐
- EMBARRASSED ☐
- EXCITED ☐
- FRIENDLY ☐
- GUILTY ☐
- HAPPY ☐
- HOPEFUL ☐
- SOLITARY ☐
- BELOVED ☐
- NERVOUS ☐
- OFFENDED ☐
- AFRAID ☐
- THOUGHTFUL ☐
- TIRED OUT ☐
- UNCOMFORTABLE ☐
- UNCERTAIN ☐

Daily Wins

DAILY MOOD CYCLE

Instructions: Think about your day from start to finish. Color the first square to express your feelings each time of the day. Next, write a word that reflects your feelings, and draw in the circle a picture of your face that reflects your feelings at that moment.

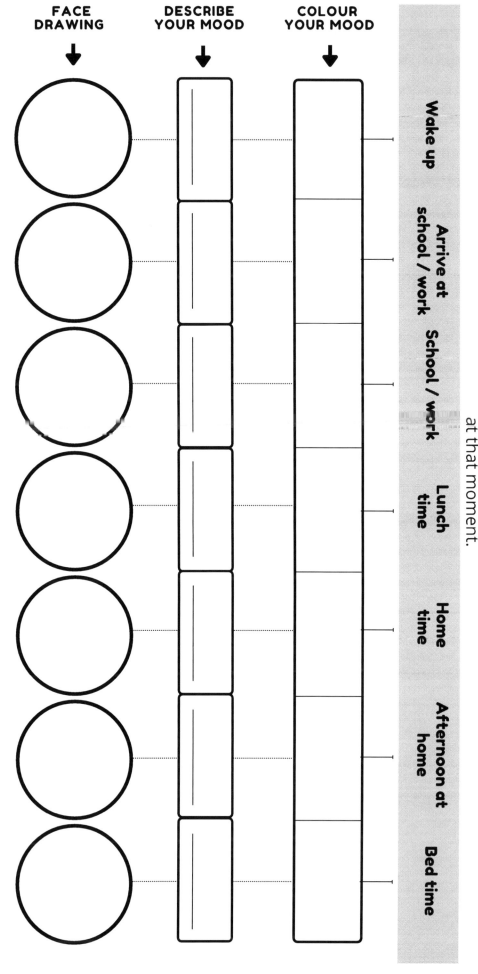

FACE DRAWING

DESCRIBE YOUR MOOD

COLOUR YOUR MOOD

Wake up

Arrive at school / work

School / work

Lunch time

Home time

Afternoon at home

Bed time

AVOIDANT ATTACHMENT WORKSHEET

Date : _____

DAILY / WEEKLY - DBT WORKSHEET (OPTIONAL)

- List three emotions that surfaced throughout yesterday. Reflect on how each emotion affected my interactions and decisions.
- Write a kind and supportive message to myself, focusing on self-acceptance and understanding.
- What are the prospects that will make you give up the difficulty of trusting others and open up.
- Write down one boundary I can set today to prioritize my emotional well-being.
- Write down any lingering worries or thoughts before bedtime, and consider ways to ease them.

_____
_____
_____
_____
_____
_____
_____
_____
_____
_____
_____
_____
_____
_____
_____
_____
_____
_____
_____

All about your journey towards changing your negative beliefs about having new romantic relationships.

_____

_____

_____

_____

_____

_____

_____

_____

_____

_____

_____

_____

_____

_____

_____

EXPOSURE THERAPY
FOR
EMOTIONAL CLOSENESS

Individuals with fearful avoidant attachment may struggle to get close to others, feel inferior to themselves and have a negative view of others.

They may avoid emotional intimacy because they see this as a threat. As someone who wants to regain their emotional balance through these exercises, try to engage in low-risk, casual interactions with others. This could mean saying hello to a neighbor or co-worker, or making small talk with a stranger.

About gradually increasing the level of intimacy over time.

	TASK ACCOMPLISHED ☐ intimacy level ○○○○○
	TASK ACCOMPLISHED ☐ intimacy level ○○○○○
	TASK ACCOMPLISHED ☐ intimacy level ○○○○○

NOTES

....

....

OVERCOMING FEARFUL AVOIDANT ATTACHMENT WORKSHEET

This table will help you examine the impact of the repercussions of the fearful avoidant attachment style on your social interactions on a daily, weekly or monthly basis... The aim of this paper is to develop an appropriate coping plan to control negative signs if you want to bring about real change in your personality.

FEARFUL AVOIDANT ATTACHMENT TAGS AND TRAITS	What are the characteristics of a fearful avoidant attachment style that you experience today? Describe how this affected your dealings.
	👍 WHAT WAS SO COOL: ✋ WHAT WAS WRONG:

AVOIDANT ATTACHMENT WORKSHEET -DBT-

START YOUR DAY MINDFULLY WITH A FEW MINUTES OF MEDITATION OR MINDFULNESS. THIS PRACTICE WILL HELP YOU FEEL CENTERED, ENHANCE SELF-AWARENESS, AND ESTABLISH A POSITIVE MINDSET FOR THE DAY.
TAKE A MOMENT TO REFLECT ON YOUR EMOTIONS AND EMOTIONAL STATE. ASK YOURSELF ABOUT YOUR FEELINGS, THOUGHTS, AND ANY ATTACHMENT-RELATED PATTERNS YOU MIGHT OBSERVE.
EMBRACE POSITIVE AFFIRMATIONS THAT FOSTER TRUST, VULNERABILITY, AND EMOTIONAL CONNECTION. REPEAT PHRASES LIKE "I AM DESERVING OF LOVE AND CONNECTION," "I AM OPEN TO EMOTIONAL INTIMACY," OR "I CAN CONFIDE IN OTHERS WITH MY FEELINGS."

✓ ___ : ___

✓ ___ : ___

Mood Tracking

- ANGRY ☐
- ANNOYED ☐
- ANXIOUS ☐
- ASHAMED ☐
- EMBARRASSING ☐
- COURAGEOUS ☐
- CALM ☐
- CHEERFUL ☐
- COLD ☐
- CONFUSED ☐
- DISCOURAGED ☐
- DISTRACTED ☐
- EMBARRASSED ☐
- EXCITED ☐
- FRIENDLY ☐
- GUILTY ☐
- HAPPY ☐
- HOPEFUL ☐
- SOLITARY ☐
- BELOVED ☐
- NERVOUS ☐
- OFFENDED ☐
- AFRAID ☐
- THOUGHTFUL ☐
- TIRED OUT ☐
- UNCOMFORTABLE ☐
- UNCERTAIN ☐

Daily Wins

DAILY MOOD CYCLE

Instructions: Think about your day from start to finish. Color the first square to express your feelings each time of the day. Next, write a word that reflects your feelings, and draw in the circle a picture of your face that reflects your feelings at that moment.

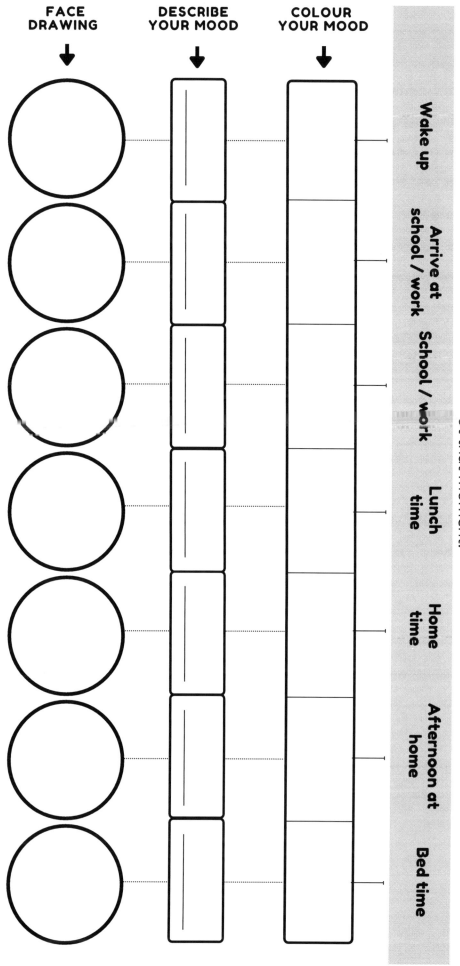

FACE DRAWING

DESCRIBE YOUR MOOD

COLOUR YOUR MOOD

Wake up

Arrive at school / work

School / work

Lunch time

Home time

Afternoon at home

Bed time

AVOIDANT ATTACHMENT WORKSHEET

Date : _____

DAILY / WEEKLY - DBT WORKSHEET (OPTIONAL)

- List three emotions that surfaced throughout yesterday. Reflect on how each emotion affected my interactions and decisions.
- Write a kind and supportive message to myself, focusing on self-acceptance and understanding.
- What are the prospects that will make you give up the difficulty of trusting others and open up.
- Write down one boundary I can set today to prioritize my emotional well-being.
- Write down any lingering worries or thoughts before bedtime, and consider ways to ease them.

All about your journey towards changing your negative beliefs about having new romantic relationships.

_____

_____

_____

_____

_____

_____

_____

_____

_____

_____

_____

_____

_____

_____

_____

Made in the USA
Middletown, DE
19 September 2023

38833766R00060